THE US CIVIL RIGHTS MOVEMENT FOR DISABILITIES

History Books America | Children's History Books

Speedy Publishing LLC

40 E. Main St. #1156

Newark, DE 19711

www.speedypublishing.com

Copyright 2017

There are many people around the world that have disabilities. They might be born with the disability or possibly became disabled due to a disease, a battle wound, or an accident. The disability rights movement became an effort protecting the civil rights of people that have a disability and to make sure that they are given the same opportunities and rights as everyone else.

PHYSICALLY DISABLED STUDENTS' PROGRAM

In 1962, Ed Roberts started a movement for Disability Rights using the Civil Rights movement as a guide, when he was carried up the stairway at the University of California at Berkeley after being lifted from his wheelchair.

They were forced to sue the government in order to prove they had the same abilities and rights to receive an education, employment, and be able to access all buildings. During this same time period, Women and Black Americans were being discriminated against as well.

While these topics were making the news, not much thought was given to people with disabilities. Roberts started a crusade at Berkeley that included a program offering help to any student 24 hours a day called the **Physically Disabled Students' Program**.

In 1972 he then took these programs into the lives of the disabled and founded the Center for Independent Living. As a non-profit organization, it was set up to assist graduates of the University that had disabilities around the area of the San Francisco Bay in finding jobs, living accommodations and any additional needs they might require. As with the Berkeley program, this one was operated and ran by disabled people and became so successful that there are now more than 300 of these centers across the United States.

His group was then joined by other people with disabilities and they protested and fought to attain the possibility of having the same rights and chances as people that did not have disabilities. It wasn't until 1992 that the Americans With Disabilities Act finally passed.

This law means that it is considered a crime to discriminate against a disabled person and makes it mandatory that all private and public buildings are accessible to people with disabilities.

Some of the required changes include doors and sidewalks need to be able to accommodate wheelchairs, buses should accommodate wheelchairs by the use of a lift, people that have visual disabilities now have braille and verbal access to cross the streets and use elevators, stairs and revolving doors now have to accommodate wheelchairs with a separate access, and schools have to accommodate children that are mentally and physically disabled.

Before implementation of this law, studies found that approximately two thirds of the disabled population were unemployed and most disabled children did not have access to an education. In the United States of America, this movement set an example for many different countries to provide respect and accessibility for their citizens and then made similar changes needed which provided disabled people to enjoy productive lives.

DISABILITY RIGHTS MOVEMENT

This movement tries to achieve standards in society so that equal opportunity is provided to disabled people. Some of these standards include equal employment, equal housing opportunities, education, safety, protection from neglect and abuse, and accessibility.

Many disabled veterans returned from World War II. Since that time, there has been a great effort to get laws passed to assist the disabled.

The three major laws passed in the last 50 years to protect the disabled consist of the Architectural Barriers Act of 1968, the Rehabilitation Act of 1973, and the Americans with Disabilities Act of 1990.

Before the laws were passed, if someone had a disability and had to be confined to a wheelchair, they were not able to even cross a street without encountering problems. They could not catch a bus, enter an office building or any other building without encountering problems.

If they had mental and physical disabilities they would often be discriminated against, even if they were more qualified than another person interviewing for the same job. They were often considered to be second class citizens by society.

The Architectural Barriers Act of 1968 regulates that all buildings have to be accessible to people that have physical disabilities. An example would be that they would have to provide an elevator or ramp in addition to stairs so that someone with a wheelchair would be able to access the building.

ВНИМАНИЕ!
ДВЕРЬ АВТОМАТИЧЕСКАЯ,
ОТКРЫВАЕТСЯ НАРУЖУ

The Rehabilitation Act of 1973 was passed to protect the education and employment rights of disabled people.

According to this law employers must consider a disabled person for a job and has to make accommodations that are considered "reasonable" to meet their needs. Currently, it also protects them from harassment on the job.

THE AMERICANS WITH DISABILITIES ACT OF 1990

The Americans with Disabilities Act of 1990 is considered as the most important disability law to date and affords them the same protection against discrimination as the Civil Rights Act of 1964 provided to people based on race, religion, and gender.

This law gives them the right to employment, public transportation, and accommodations in public facilities. It also provided regulations including public restrooms, handicapped parking, braille, and more.

2 DOWNT
DALL
QUEEN LATIFAH SEPT. 16
011
WEEKDAYS
2PM
DART

Under the guidance of the ADA, a disability is defined as being "a physical or mental impairment that substantially limits a major life activity."

It then goes on to define a few of these activities as caring for oneself, performing manual tasks, seeing, hearing, eating, walking, lifting, speaking, reading, thinking, working, communicating, etc. If the condition can be corrected, a person is not considered to be disabled.

An example would be that since it might be possible to correct a person's vision, then they would not be considered as disabled because of limited vision.

THE AMERICANS WITH DISABILITIES ACT AMENDMENTS ACT OF 2008

This act was signed by the President on September 25, 2008 as Public Law 110-325, becoming effective January 1, 2009. Its emphasis is how a disability is defined and favors a greater coverage of people as permitted by the terms of the original Act and does not require an extensive analysis.

President George H.W. Bush signs the Americans With Disabilities Act into law.

It also makes changes defining "disability" by rejecting holdings of many Supreme Court rulings and part of the EEOC's original regulations included in the ADA. These changes make it easier for a disabled person who seeks protection under the rules of the ADA to establish that they have a disability under the rules of the ADA.

This regulation also requires that it is easier for individuals seeking coverage under "disability" in the "regarded as" section. Previously it was difficult for people to obtain coverage under this "regarded as" section. Under the amendments, the focus relates as to how a disabled person may have been treated due to their impairment, rather than what the employer felt regarding the impairment of the individual.

However, these regulations clarify than a disabled person is provided coverage under its first prong, "actual disability", so as to be qualified for an accommodation that is considered reasonable.

They also state that generally it is not required to move on to the first and second prongs if that person does not challenge the employer's failure in not providing a reasonable accommodation.

THE AMERICAN CIVIL LIBERTIES RIGHTS UNION

This organization strives that America be free of discrimination against disabled people, they value individuals with disabilities, its members are united and have access to homes, education, employment, health care and families.

zin
QUICKIE

They are committed to making surethatdisabledindividualsare not segregated in institutions such as psychiatric hospitals, nursing homes, prisons, and jails. The ACLU has been around over 100 years.

FAMOUS PEOPLE THAT ARE DISABLED

There have been several disabled people that you may have heard about. They are our leaders, heroes, scientists, athletes, entertainers, to name a few. Here is a listing of some disabled people that are well-known:

Jim Abbott was born without his right hand, but was able to overcome his disability to become became a baseball pitcher in the major-league.

Ludwig van Beethoven was one of the most well-known music composers in history, even being deaf for much of his career.

Ray Charles was a well-known singer/songwriter that was totally blind by the time he turned seven.

Stephen Hawking is one of the greatest recognized scientists of individuals. After being diagnosed with ALS, he then became paralyzed. He uses a computer to communicate.

Helen Keller became blind and deaf when she was young which resulted from a fever. She persisted and learned to talk as well as to learn braille. She was even able to write about her life experiences.

Christopher Reeve, known for playing Superman on the big screen, as well as many other movies, became paralyzed when he fell while riding a horse. He then advocated for the people with similar spinal-cord injuries.

President Franklin D. Roosevelt, while he recovered from polio, lost his ability to walk without assistance.

If you want to find out more information about Disability Rights be sure to go to your local library, research on the internet, and ask questions of your teachers, family and friends.

Visit

BABY PROFESSOR
EDUCATION KIDS

www.BabyProfessorBooks.com

to download Free Baby Professor eBooks
and view our catalog of new and exciting
Children's Books

www.ingramcontent.com/pod-product-compliance
Lightning Source LLC
Chambersburg PA
CBHW081235130726

47997CB00009B/2882

9 798869 430038